W.C. Handy

Father Of The Blues

Alice Yeager

Seacoast Publishing
Birmingham, Alabama

Published by Seacoast Publishing, Inc.
1149 Mountain Oaks Drive
Birmingham, Alabama 35226

Library of Congress Control Number: 2002112973

Cover art by Thomas B. Moore

ISBN 1-878561-51-0

To obtain copies of this book, please write or call:
Seacoast Publishing, Inc.
Post Office Box 26492
Birmingham, Alabama 35260
(205) 979-2909

Dedication

To my family who supports everything I pursue.

To my friends who offer encouragement at just the right moments.

To Pam Tanner, my "technology buddy,"
what would I have done without you?

To Mrs. Pearley Woods, my new friend,
for her gracious help on this project.

And to Tim . . . everybody needs a "Tim" in their life.

About The Series

Alabama Roots is a book series designed to provide reading pleasure for young people, to allow readers to better know the men and women who shaped the State of Alabama, and to fill a much-needed void of quality regional non-fiction for students in middle grades.

For years, teachers and librarians have searched for quality biographies about famous people from Alabama. This series is a response to that search. The series will cover a span of time from pre-statehood through the modern day.

The goal of *Alabama Roots* is to provide biographies that are historically accurate and as interesting as the characters whose lives they explore.

The *Alabama Roots* mark assures readers and educators of consistent quality in research, composition, and presentation.

It is a joint publishing project of Seacoast Publishing, Inc., and Will Publishing, Inc., both located in Birmingham, Alabama.

Alice Yeager

How I Wrote This Book

There were several things to be done before I could begin to write down my thoughts on paper. I started by visiting the W.C. Handy Museum in Florence, Alabama. This is my hometown so I made several visits to the museum. Mrs. Pearley Woods, the museum's curator, was a tremendous help. I toured the cabin and looked through artifacts and pictures donated by the Handy family. Mrs. Woods shared lots of information and she even played a recording of W.C. Handy's own voice telling about growing up and wanting to be a musician so badly. I visited the library located next to the museum and looked through articles and books from the library's special collection. These cannot be checked out so I made several pages of notes.

I purchased a copy of Handy's autobiography that was published in 1941. The book was a wonderful source of information because it was written by Mr. Handy himself. After reading and re-reading passages, I began to get ideas for my book.

When I typed W.C. Handy's name on the Internet, there were over 15,000 entries! This was great because there were lots of sources to look at, but looking at so many took awhile! I began to realize that most of the information from the sources was actually what I had learned from the autobiography. There was little new information. I also read several books on the history of Florence to complete my research. This helped to answer questions about the town and its people during the time that W.C. Handy lived in this area.

I sketched a rough outline and then started listing the important events in W.C. Handy's life into a logical sequence. I had pages of notes, so many that I couldn't possibly use all the things that I had written. Deciding what to leave out was difficult, but necessary.

I wrote, and re-wrote, and re-wrote. I read my story over and over to check for mistakes and to get it just the way I wanted it. I submitted my work to an editor who helped develop the finished product.

Finally, I wanted to add photographs to the book, so I called Mr. Handy's family in New York. I spoke several times with Ms. Minnie Handy Hanson, the President of Handy Brothers Music Company, Inc. Ms. Hanson helped by identifying people in the pictures and by telling me when the pictures were made. She also granted permission for the pictures to be used.

Writing this book took a lot of time and hard work, but the thrill of actually seeing it on a library's bookshelf will make all my efforts worthwhile!

—*Alice Yeager*

Contents

Introduction

The world knows W.C. Handy as "The Father of the Blues" but no one is quicker than Mr. Handy to point out that he did not *invent* the blues.

He just happened to notice the music that was hiding in sounds from everyday life in northwest Alabama and Mississippi and Tennessee that others took for granted. Others may have noticed the sounds too. But W.C. Handy was the first person to ever take those sounds and turn them into a new kind of music.

Most important, it was a new sound that seemed to touch the heart and soul of everybody who heard it.

It was this new sound that lifted W.C. Handy from a cabin on an Alabama hill to extraordinary heights of stardom as one of the world's most famous musicians.

There were two main parts to Handy's great success.

First, he saw the musical possibilities in everyday

sounds that others just heard as noise. He listened carefully to the sounds that came from laborers as they tried to make their daily chores bearable and the sometimes happy, sometimes sad, songs of back street beer joint musicians. He heard the music of water in a brook rippling over stones, the chirp of birds, and the grunts and calls from animals deep in the woods.

Second, Handy collected those sounds and stashed them away in his mind even as a child. He remembered the melodies of the labor songs, and wrote down the words of the beer joint musicians. He taught himself to make those same sounds with musical instruments.

He played with songs all his life, adding new sounds and subtracting others.

Handy blended the sounds of life into a new kind of symphony. It was a symphony not for fancy and rich people, although many of them liked the new music too.

Handy's music was a symphony for everyday folks. The people who loved it first and most were those who had to work the hardest and got paid the least. They were people with broken hearts and broken dreams. They were the people who always hoped for a better life, but never really believed they would find it.

It was music that captured their hopes and dreams and frustrations and failures. And through the sweet and soulful sounds that W.C. Handy captured, his music made their lives a little bit better.

They were common Alabama sounds, captured by a common Alabama boy—a boy with an uncommon ear that could hear things that no one else noticed. And he turned those common sounds into the most uncommon music that all the world loved to hear.

His music was called *the blues.*

Another Minister?

IT WAS THE MIDDLE OF NOVEMBER, the time of year when sharp northwest winds blow down the Tennessee River Valley and bring a damp chill that can sink all the way to the bone.

Those sharp winds also bring heavy clouds and rain that washes away the bright Indian Summer days of early fall, and make the whole valley look sad.

But on one particular November day in a little northwest Alabama cabin, no amount of wind or rain or gloomy skies could change the bright happiness inside.

It was the home of Reverend Charles B. Handy and on this day he was just about as happy as he had ever been in his life.

In his arms he held his new baby boy. He stared deeply into the tiny face and he smiled a big, broad smile.

The baby did not smile back. The baby was *not*

happy.

In fact, the baby was crying his tiny lungs out.

Preacher Handy didn't care. His faced glowed with joy and pride. The *wah, wah, wah* of his new son's cry didn't bother him one bit.

Reverend Charles B. Handy, William's father

Preacher Handy was so proud that nothing else mattered right then. "This child's got a fine set of lungs, yes siree," said Reverend Handy as the baby wailed. "He's got a mighty fine, strong set of lungs. Why I do believe that one of these days he'll be quite a preacher!"

It was November 16, 1873. William Christopher Handy came into the world screaming. He was born with gassy stomach pains, and cried with them for six straight months. Many babies have the stomach pains, known as colic.

The crying seemed to never stop, but Reverend Handy never seemed to mind. Each time little William cried out, his father just took it as a sign that one day his son would use these same vocal cords to shout out from a church pulpit.

Charles and Elizabeth Brewer Handy knew that life for William, their first baby, would be far different from their own lives. They had been released from slavery only a few years before William's birth. William would be owned by no man, as they had been. He would have the chance to make his own way in the world.

It was only natural that the minute young William was born, everyone assumed he would be a preacher some day. His father and his grandfather were well-known Methodist preachers. And his mother's family faithfully attended the nearby Baptist Church.

Surely he would become a fine, dignified minister just like his father and grandfather.

Young William surely was destined to become a preacher of the gospel.

Life On Handy's Hill

FLORENCE IS IN THE EXTREME NORTHWEST corner of Alabama, just south of Tennessee and only a stone's throw to Mississippi from the city's western edge. The Tennessee River flows along the southern edge of town and broad fields of rich farm land spread both north and south from the river.

The fact that the Tennessee River was shallow—its water flowing swiftly over a shallow rocky bottom—was a big reason that Florence became a village. Riverboats could go up the Tennessee River from the wide shallow area, known as shoals. And they could go down the river from the shoals. But they couldn't cross the shoals. The boats would have to be loaded and unloaded to get their cargo up and down the river.

When the riverboats stopped for loading and unloading, there had to be people to do the work.

There also had to be places for the boat crewmen and boat passengers to eat, sleep and shop.

Some businessmen noticed that northwest Alabama was a pretty place where crops grew easily, and decided it could be much more than a place to load and unload boats. In 1818, a year before Alabama became a state, they bought 5,000 acres around the little village and began building a real town. They picked out a spot for a college, a school for women, a park, a market and a courthouse. They built wide streets. Then they advertised for people to come and live in the new town.

People came from all around to live in the new town. Many of them felt lucky to have the chance to live in such a nice new place.

The Handys, however, ended up in this river town in a hard-luck sort of way. William's grandfather—William Wise Handy—was a runaway slave who was kidnapped while on the run from his master and sold into Alabama.

When the slaves were freed at the end of the Civil War, Grandfather Handy stayed in Alabama and became the first black man to own property in Florence and he built the first church there for black people. He also helped start several other churches for black people in northwest Alabama.

Two miles north of the Tennessee River the flat farm land rises gradually to form a hill, just outside town. It is a tall hill, the tallest in the area. It was surrounded by woods and bounded on one side by the cold waters of Cypress Creek. Miles of woods and farms could be seen from the top of the hill. It was here on this high ground that the Handy family built their home.

It came to be known as Handy's Hill.

William's father and grandfather chopped down trees from the hill to build their home. William's grandfather chopped and straightened the logs for the Handy cabin. With a small hatchet he shaved the logs so smooth that they fit together snugly as he stacked them into walls. William's father carefully beat down the kitchen's dirt floor so that it felt like stone against bare feet.

The snug little cabin kept the family warm when cold, wet winter winds swept freezing rains and snow down the Tennessee Valley. It kept them dry when heavy spring rains pounded the tin roof.

The small cabin sat in the middle of a three-acre orchard of cherries, pears, damsons, and quinces. The orchard and surrounding woods and fields were home to many birds and small animals, each with its own place and own sound.

High rocky cliffs overlooked one side of the woodland. Cypress Creek protected the other and offered catfish, perch, trout and an abundant supply of eels for the Handy table.

It was on this hill that Charles and Elizabeth Brewer Handy raised their son. It was where young William played in the orchard, woods and creek, and it was where Charles practiced his sermons and lived a stern and conservative Christian life.

He believed in hard work and clean living. His

The home where W.C. Handy grew up is in Florence, and is on the grounds of the W.C. Handy Museum

rules for clean living included not allowing music to be played. Reverend Handy believed that music, if it was not church music, was the devil's work. He had no intention of allowing music in his home.

Handy Hill was a great place for a boy to grow up.

William visited Cypress Creek and watched turtles sun themselves on rocks and driftwood until drizzling rain made them dive into the water. He laughed to see turtles plopping into the creek to avoid getting wet in the rain.

He tiptoed with quick caution around the creek banks. He knew that water moccasins, rattlesnakes, and other scary animals lived along the creek. While he was afraid of them, he didn't let it stop him from wandering the woods and streams. He was a good shot with a rock and was quick to throw at anything that slithered.

The icy waters of Cypress Creek made a perfect swimming hole on hot summer days. William watched his cousins and other kids from Handy's Hill splash and swim in the cool waters and wanted to join in. His father had carried William to the nearby Tennessee River and tried to teach him to swim. But no matter what Reverend Handy tried, young William just couldn't stay afloat. Reverend Handy finally gave up and they headed home.

However, William was determined to swim and so he decided there was only one way to do it. One day when no one else was around, he jumped into the treacherous Blue Hole of Cypress Creek. The water was way over his head. Luckily, William came up swimming!

William loved the times that his grandparents and parents told old stories about their families. He always sat close and listened to the hard times of slavery days, and the funny things that had happened to his family.

He heard very different stories of slavery days from his grandfather Handy and his grandfather Christopher Brewer, his mother's father.

Everyone knew Grandfather Handy's story of his running away to find freedom, of being kidnapped and sold back into slavery in Alabama. But the story that made them gasp was the one about Grandfather Handy's son, Hanson, who was William's uncle.

The Handy's were owned by a mean plantation owner who decided one day to whip young Hanson. Hanson refused to be whipped so the owner sold him away from his family to a man in Arkansas. No one in the family ever saw Hanson after the day he was sold away. The family was proud of Hanson's bravery, but William's father always cried when the church choir sang *March Along, I'll See You on the Judgement Day.* It was the song that the slaves sang the day Hanson was sold away.

Grandpa Brewer's story was different. Even when Grandpa Brewer was given his freedom from his owner, John Wilson, he decided to remain as Wilson's servant.

One day robbers came to the Wilson house and tortured Wilson so he would tell them where his money was hidden. He never told and the robbers killed him.

Next they attacked Grandpa Brewer, but he wouldn't tell either, even when they tortured him, shot him and threatened to kill him. After he healed from his wounds, he went to Nashville, Tennessee, where Wilson's son lived and told them where the family's money was hidden.

William was proud of both grandfathers, and he was even more proud that he had been named for them. *William* for Grandpa Handy. *Christopher* for Grandpa Brewer.

Uncle Mose Brewer had a story about an old

rooster that William loved to hear. Uncle Mose always broke into a big grin when he told about William's father and Uncle Buck Brewer coming to spend a weekend in the country with him.

"Now those two fellows loved to eat! They both had appetites that took a backseat to nobody. One Saturday these two headed out to my house for an overnight visit. Now it just so happened that I had an ornery old rooster that ruled the barnyard from his perch on the back fence. He never left that throne except to knock off a younger rival or perhaps to say 'howdy' to a hen. That old bird was much too tough to eat, and he seemed to know it. He was always passed over when it was time for Sunday stew or good ol' fried chicken with gravy."

"Well now, on this particular weekend, I was in a quandary," Uncle Mose went on. "How was I going to supply three Sunday meals, plus Monday breakfast, to these two heavy-eating guests? Finally I decided that the old rooster had to go. I got my hatchet and started toward the barnyard. But wouldn't you know—for the first time in years that ol' rooster couldn't be found. The day passed, and no rooster. Sunday came and passed. Monday dawned. Still no bird. About noon everybody packed up and left. As soon as they were safely out of sight that devilish ol' rooster strolled nonchalantly out of the nearby woods, returned to his customary place on the fence and distinctly crowed, 'Is H-a-n-d-y gone?'"

Grandma Handy's name was Thumuthis. She was kind hearted and always generous to young William. She often gave him money, but she always turned her back when she took the money out of her pocketbook so William couldn't see inside. It was just one of the little lessons that she liked to teach—that some things are private matters and the handling of money was one of them.

Grandma Thumuthis was a dark-skinned, proudly handsome woman and walked as straight and regally as a queen. She was the family doctor, patching wounds and curing many different ills with her home remedies. She often cured fevers with the juice of mashed peach leaves. Mullein tea and Jimson weeds were used for swellings, sassafras tea was used to thin blood, catnip tea was brewed to cure hives, while the marrow from hog jowls was her specialty for the mumps. She used sheep manure to brew tea when family members came down with the measles. They called it *nanny tea*, and it tasted as bad as it sounds. Once while William was battling a severe sore throat, Grandma Thumuthis made him gargle with his own urine. No one dared to question Grandma Thumuthis' remedies—after all, *somehow* everyone she doctored managed to survive.

William loved his grandma for many reasons, but he liked her most for what she said about his big ears: she believed they were a sign that he had a talent for music.

"Child, those big ears of yours are just perfect for listening to music . . . you listen carefully with those big ears and you'll hear things most of us might just miss out on."

Every time she said it, William adored her even more.

Grandma Thumuthis was the only one in his world who encouraged his secret love for music. In fact, musical instruments were considered the devil's playthings and one uncle even forbid his sons to whistle!

Once, William's mother whispered to him that she liked guitar music, but she could not play it because the church did not allow such instruments. William wondered if the fact that she liked music had anything to do with the fact that her family was Baptist, instead of Methodist like his father. Usually the family went to the Methodist Church. But once in a while William and his mother visited the Baptist Church. When they did, it was easy for him to see the difference in how each group worshiped. He like the way that the Baptists patted their feet and swayed from side to side when they sang. He watched his mother and knew that she might be going to the Methodist Church, but in her heart she still was a shoutin' Baptist. She had rhythm in her blood and sometimes she just had to shout and sway.

Grandpa Brewer seemed to be the only other relative who even slightly enjoyed music. And that was only *before* he got religion. When he was a young man in slavery days, he played the fiddle for dances to make extra money. His master allowed him to keep the money. "Oh, how the folks knew when it was time for the music to get hot!" Grandpa Brewer said. "They had their own way of bearing down. A boy would stand behind the fiddler with a pair of knitting needles in his hands. Then the youngster would reach around the fiddler's left shoulder and beat on the strings in the manner of a snare drummer."

William saw a glimpse of excitement in Grandpa Brewer's eyes when he told about the old ways of making rhythm. But Grandpa always ended by saying that he had given up such sinful doings once he got religion.

Young Handy wished that there could be more talk about music, but it wasn't going to happen.

Lessons Of Life

CHARLES HANDY HAD A PREACHING STYLE all his own. Just about everyone who heard him agreed that he could preach a fine sermon. But he preached in a different style than the other preachers. He read the Bible and preached quietly and reverently. The other black preachers in town shouted and stomped. While other preachers decked themselves in bright clothes and wore gold watch chains around their necks, Charles Handy dressed simply.

Even though his style was different, just about everyone in Florence loved and admired Reverend Handy. William couldn't help but notice how everyone treated his father well. People would tip their hats and stop to speak to William and his father whenever they walked downtown.

With his father being a preacher, young William spent many hours going to church, not just on Sundays, but prayer meetings and revivals too.

It was at one of those revivals that William found himself sitting by an old man with watery eyes. The old man looked over at William and said, "You's old enough to think 'bout yo' dyin' days, son."

William didn't like what the man said. He didn't know what to say. But he did think about it, and at the next revival meeting he sat right down with the mourners on the bench to "get religion." The preacher preached and the singers sang. William listened solemnly, and watched as one by one the others he was sitting with spoke up about being saved and feeling the spirit of God in their hearts. But William felt nothing. He wondered if something was wrong with him that he didn't feel the spirit.

His father could tell that William was concerned.

Back at home his father came to William and said, "It's not *getting* religion, Sonny; it's *doing* religion that counts."

A few weeks later a group of black people passed in front of the Handy cabin. They were on their way to Africa. They had decided that returning to Africa was better than fighting the poor treatment they were getting from the white people in America. They left their homes in the snow with little more than the clothes on their backs. And for many of them, those clothes were just rags. One small boy was barefoot. William and his father watched as they passed. Reverend Handy could see on William's face the pain he felt for the cold and weary people.

"Sonny," he asked William, "do you want to give that boy your shoes and stockings?"

"Yes," William quickly replied. "I'd like to."

Reverend Handy called to the group, asking them to wait. William removed his shoes and stockings and handed them to the young stranger. The child's look of gratitude warmed William's heart. Then the group started off again. Watching them slowly fade into the snowy haze, William suddenly realized what his father meant when he said that *doing* religion was more important than *getting* religion.

William's father admired people with good character and paid particular attention to the way good citizens acted. He told young William what he saw in those people and suggested that William could also learn some good lessons by watching how good citizens behaved.

William and his father often walked by the old Exchange Hotel. It was the place where Edward A. O'Neal came to talk with friends about government and politics. O'Neal lived in Florence and had been governor of Alabama from 1882 to 1886. Many people in Florence still called him governor, even though he wasn't governor any longer.

Governor O'Neal was as good at giving a speech as Reverend Handy was at preaching a sermon, maybe even better. He was so good that sometimes when he was at the hotel talking, people gathered to listen.

William and his father often stopped to hear the governor talk about political news of the day. They were impressed by Governor O'Neal's forceful way of talking as he presided over the discussions. He was so interesting that sometimes a crowd would listen for a long time while the governor just read the newspaper aloud. Reverend Handy pointed out to William little things about Governor O'Neal—his little gestures and the way he spoke, things that many people never noticed.

"Now Sonny, you could learn from this man. Just you look. All eyes are on this fellow and the crowd is hanging on his *every* word."

William paid close attention. He was as impressed as everyone else with the former governor.

While William respected Governor O'Neal, there other important white people in Alabama who said bad things about black people. Their words made

William angry. Many leaders encouraged Southerners to prevent black people from getting a good education, and to give them jobs only as cooks, nursemaids, mechanics and farmers. After listening to one particularly cruel speech from the courthouse steps, William ran home, buried his head in his pillow and cried so hard that he couldn't stop for a long time. The speaker was a politician running for office. He said that money spent to educate black children was a waste. If the citizens elected him, he promised not to waste the state's money on such things.

William finally stopped crying. He picked himself up and ran into the woods where he gave his own speech to the trees and the animals of the thicket. He yelled in his loudest voice and argued against each of the speechmaker's points. He liked the words, his very own words, that bravely echoed back through the forest to him. He slept well that night because he knew that man was wrong, and he knew why.

He might not be a preacher, but young William was discovering that he sure had the voice and the passion and the ability to think and say what he felt.

Elizabeth Brewer Handy watched her young William grow up and felt the pride in her heart. He was intelligent and gentle and caring, yet strong and willing to stand up against things that were wrong. She knew that her William was special.

Elizabeth was the youngest of six children and had been called “Babe” by her family. No one but family members could call her Babe and she tolerated no name other than “William” for her son. Names were special to Elizabeth.

She believed that a good name showed strength of character. She had chosen the name William Christopher Handy for her baby boy, giving him the names of his grandfathers—respected men—and with the name came a responsibility to honor their good names.

Though shy and gentle, Elizabeth could stand her ground when her pride was threatened.

One afternoon an important white woman in Florence stopped William and asked him to deliver baskets of vegetables that she had fixed for her friends and customers. Obediently William began making the deliveries. The more trips he made, the more the woman asked William to make. The afternoon began to slip away with no end in sight for the errands, so William refused to deliver any more baskets. He explained to the woman that he was hungry and his mother always expected him to come straight home from school. The woman insisted on more deliveries and gave William a buttered biscuit to soothe his hunger and a dime to pay for the deliveries.

When William finally got home, his mother was frantic with worry. Her worry changed to anger when he explained why he was late. She grabbed her bonnet, and ordered, "William, you come with me."

William followed his mother to the home of the woman who had insisted that William make deliveries for her. Never again was William to be sent on errands without her permission, Mrs. Handy told the woman. "As for the biscuit," she added emphatically, "he has better at home."

Tears welled up in the woman's eyes. She had meant no harm, she said. But Mrs. Handy's message was clear: Black children get hungry just like white children, and a black child's mother gets just as worried as a white child's mother when the child doesn't come home on time.

One Sunday morning the Handy family borrowed a buggy and rode out from Florence to worship with their country cousins. William looked spiffy and he knew it! His mother had tailored a fluted waist top, embroidered it with lace, and ironed it ever so carefully. He also wore gleaming, red-topped, brass-toed boots and a sailor suit.

William laughed at the dreary country boys perched like crows on a rail fence as the buggy neared the small country church. The boys wore long shirts made of flour sacks and nothing more.

William's father explained that as a young boy in slavery days he had dressed much the same way—long shirttails and no pants. William's mother frowned as her son snickered at the country boys. All of a sudden she called to the youngsters. The horse stopped, and the boys timidly ambled to the buggy. *What was going on?* William wondered.

"Who is your mother, boys?" Mrs. Handy asked.

As they answered, Mrs. Handy turned to William and said, "These are your third cousins." William's puffed out chest quickly went flat. These raggedy kids were his kinfolks! He certainly got the point that his mother intended.

Music Everywhere

JUST ABOUT ALL THE KIDS around Handy's Hill loved baseball. A game was started every time enough of them could get loose from their chores to make two teams.

William played too, but it wasn't his favorite thing.

His eyes were sensitive to the bright sun, and he squinted to see. The other players called him "squinch-eyed monkey" and it hurt his feelings.

Then one day he missed a hard throw. It whacked him hard in the right eye, and made him see stars.

William decided that baseball was not for him.

After that, when the other boys gathered to play ball, he slipped into the deep woods where it was shadier and he didn't have to squint, and where the forest sounds were music to his ears.

William could tell every different sound of the

field, forest and river even before he was ten years old, and he could find music in every sound. He knew the different whistle of each riverboat floating down the Tennessee River. He could identify every bird in the orchard by listening to their songs. Even the bellow of the bull became a musical note.

William could close his eyes and see music notes on a scale as he listened to a bird's tender love chirp and the answering call of its mate. Robins warbled a warm alto while bobolinks were quite the opposite. Mocking birds sang another unique tone. He distinctly heard a French horn from the breast of the blue jay. The tappings of the woodpecker became a snare drum. The bullfrog's call made a perfect bass for his choir.

A million crickets chimed in as darkness descended on Handy's Hill. The katydids also offered a soothing sound each summer's night. The moo of cows lumbering in from the fields sounded just like a saxophone, while the moody whippoorwills were a clarinet. William listened intently to the sounds of his world and pretended that he was the conductor of this outdoor orchestra.

He catalogued each sound. He had gotten the habit of carefully keeping track of things by watching his father. William noticed that when his father loaned someone a hoe or other garden tool, he listed it in a book as if it were money.

Reverend Handy also wrote down the name and date of each family birth and death. Like his father, William listed the things that were important to him. But he didn't need a notebook. Each sound was tucked away in his mind, never to be lost or forgotten.

Every time William heard a sound, he just had to find a way to make the sound himself. After listening to the trumpet player with the Baptist choir, he didn't rest until he found an old cow horn. He hollowed out the horn and cut off the pointed end for a mouthpiece. It didn't sound exactly like the real thing, but each time he blew into the old cow horn, his music sounded just fine to him.

William turned all sorts of things into musical instruments. One day when he was roaming the woods in search of treasures he found the jawbone of a long-dead horse. He showed the other kids on Handy's Hill how to make rhythm by scraping a twenty-penny nail across the teeth of the jawbone. A broom handle and a jug became grand additions to his band. The children giggled as William showed them how to change their voices while singing through fine-toothed combs. He taught them to place the thumb of the left hand under their chins to make strange sounds as they rattled their teeth. Sometimes they would place the right hand's thumb on their Adam's apple, and yell verses like:

Went down the river
Couldn't get across
Paid five dollars for an old gray horse.

Making instruments was great fun for William, and even his mother went along with it as she loaned him her tin pans and milk pails for drums.

But music, real music, wasn't allowed.

To Reverend Handy, if it wasn't church music, it was the devil's work.

Sooner or later, there was going to be a problem.

Something Special

WILLIAM'S FATHER HAD MANY SAYINGS about life. He used them all the time in his sermons. The one repeated most often in the Handy household was "An idle brain is the devil's workshop."

What he meant was that if everyone in the family worked hard and stayed busy, the devil couldn't come along and tempt them with thoughts of evil doing.

Most of the time, it was good advice.

For William, it was another story.

William never minded hard work.

During the spring and summer months he picked berries and sold fruit from the orchard. He gathered and sold chestnuts, walnuts and hickory nuts during the fall. He also learned to make lye-soap.

Reverend Handy made William divide the money he earned into three equal parts. One part he got to keep. One part he gave to Reverend Handy. One part he gave to his mother. From his part, William was required to drop a dime in the church collection plate each Sunday and save a nickel for Sunday School. Usually he made no more than three dollars a week, so there wasn't much left after his money was portioned out and he gave his church offering.

Reverend Handy was proud of his hard-working son. One warm day he kept William home from school. They visited a neighboring field where a mule and a plow waited in the hot sunshine. Reverend Handy placed the reins in William's hands and explained how to plow with a mule. "Now to a mule 'gee' means go to the right and 'haw' means go to the left. Let's see you give it a try."

William tried his best to maneuver the stubborn beast, but the mule was doing a better job of maneuvering William.

"Sonny, I hope you won't have to do this for a living," said Reverend Handy, "but the work sure won't hurt you."

William sensed that his father wanted him to work with his mind instead of laboring long hours in the scorching Alabama fields. The plowing was just a lesson for William to know how hard it was to work the fields.

When he was twelve William earned fifty cents a day working as a water boy at a nearby rock quarry. He heard something there that he had not heard before. It was work songs; sung by the workers to help pass the time and make the job easier to endure. William liked the songs, and joined in as they chanted:

"Oh, baby, 'member las' winter?
Wasn't it cold-hunh?
Wasn't it cold-hunh?"

The *hunh* was a musical grunt made as the workers struck the steel with their hammers, tugged on a line, or lifted heavy objects.

William also worked at the McNabb iron furnace where he shoveled iron ore. He worked twelve hours every day, with a few breaks to rest. The laborers would pass the time by making music during these rare breaks. They would make a tune by beating their shovels against iron buggies, altering the tone by striking the metal at different points of contact. Sometimes a dozen men would beat their shovels in rhythm. William loved the sound.

Other jobs followed. Plastering. Shoemaking. Carpentry. Farm hand. Printer. Janitor. He bought his

A young William

own clothes, books and school supplies.

It was hard work, just the kind of hard work that Reverend Handy believed would keep William's brain from becoming idle.

But one day William's hard work carried him in a direction that Reverend Handy never expected.

It was late one afternoon. William was walking past a Florence department store when he glimpsed something that made his heart beat faster, something that made him want to work even harder. Even though he had precious little money left at the end of each week, this thing that caught his eye instantly gave him a purpose to save every precious penny.

It was a guitar. And it was a beauty!

From the minute he saw the bright and shiny instrument, he decided that he must have it. William knew that his parents frowned on musical instruments, but if he paid for it with his own money—his hard earned money—surely they would allow it and be proud that he had saved for it.

William passed by the store every day just to gaze at the guitar through the shop window. Days passed slower than cold molasses.

William was working harder than ever but told no one about his plan to buy the guitar. There was no one to tell. He had no one to share his excitement with. No one who would understand just how much getting this guitar meant to him.

It didn't matter.

He loved that guitar, and knowing that he would buy it some day was enough to make him happy.

Finally William had the exact amount needed for his precious guitar.

He proudly walked into the store and poured a bag of coins onto the counter. The clerk was not pleased to count out each small coin but to his surprise, young William had exactly enough money to buy the guitar.

William clutched the instrument tightly under his arm as he raced for home.

Wonderful and exciting visions raced through his mind.

With his new guitar William would finally be able

to express the things he heard and felt through sounds.

His feet seemed to be lifted by tiny wings and his heart was as carefree and light as a feather. He could hardly wait to reach home and show his parents just how all his hard work had paid off.

He could just see the envy on the faces of the other youngsters who lived on Handy's Hill. They would gather around, eyes popping out with curiosity and admiration, and, oh, what a hit he would be with all the young ladies.

The Devil's Plaything

WILLIAM BURST THROUGH THE CABIN DOOR so proud, happy and excited that he could not speak.

He just held up the shining instrument for everyone to admire.

But no one was smiling. Not even a little bit.

William's mother and father were speechless too.

But not from being happy.

William knew in an instant that there was trouble.

Finally William was the first to find his voice: "Look at it shine and it belongs to me. *Me!* I saved up the money."

Silence.

There was just silence.

William waited and hoped that the scene would change and his parents would congratulate him.

He wanted them to be as excited as he was.

Reverend Handy was angry.

"A box," he gasped, while William's mother stood frozen. "A guitar! One of the devil's playthings. Take it away. Take it away, I tell you. Get it out of your hands. Whatever possessed you to bring a sinful thing like that into our Christian home? Take it back where it came from. You hear?"

William was stunned. He hugged the guitar closely. His father's words sounded dim and far away like something spoken in a dream, a terribly bad dream.

William wanted to beg his father to reconsider, but he knew better. There was no changing his father's mind once it was set. Not only was William's young heart crushed because his parents were not proud for him, but they were disappointed in him for bringing a guitar into their Christian home.

"I hear what you say, and I understand what you mean," William stammered, "but I don't think they'll take it back."

"They'll exchange it!" Reverend Handy stormed without hesitating. "For the price of a thing like that you could get a new Webster's Unabridged Dictionary—something that'll do you some good."

William obeyed his father and dragged himself back to the store.

He exchanged his prized possession for the dictionary. It didn't seem like a fair exchange to him . . . a shiny guitar or a dictionary . . . there was no doubt in William's mind that he was getting a raw deal!

At the cabin, Reverend and Mrs. Handy knew they had broken William's heart.

It was not something that they wanted to do.

They talked about what to do next.

Maybe there was a way to encourage his interest in music, the right kind of music, without sacrificing their Christian principles.

They came up with an idea.

Reverend Handy enrolled William in organ lessons.

Ruth A. Jones taught him on an old Estey organ. He was a quick learner and William began arranging choral parts for church groups by the time he reached his teenage years.

Reverend Handy occasionally dropped in to hear how his son was progressing in music. *Sacred music.*

School Days

LEARNING CAME EASY for William at the Florence District School for Negroes, but his favorite part of the day was the first half-hour each morning.

While other classes started their day with Bible devotionals, William's class started with music. His teacher, Professor Y.A. Wallace, started each day with singing and music, one of the professor's favorite hobbies.

Professor Wallace would blow a note on his pitch pipe. Each student hummed his own starting pitch and the musical drills began. The daily lessons helped William understand the basics of music. He eagerly soaked in each lesson.

Professor Wallace was an odd sort of fellow. At least the people of Florence thought so. He came to the North Alabama area after graduating in the first class at Fisk University in Nashville, Tennessee, and always was a preachy sort of fellow.

William's unusual teacher, Professor Y.A. Wallace

Some people laughed at his "sermons," but he didn't seem to mind.

Professor Wallace particularly liked to rant about unhealthy eating habits.

He repeatedly reminded his students that more people died each year from overeating than from starvation. The students held in their giggles as the professor squinted his eyes, pointed his finger and declared, "overeating will be the end of many of you, just you wait and see!"

He frowned each time he saw the students' tin pails filled with lunches that were washed down with quarts of milk. His lunch each day consisted of one baked potato, sliced and buttered. At home he ate only roasted peanuts, parched corn, and dried persimmons.

Professor Wallace had little patience with his students and William had been scolded and whipped with a hickory stick more than once. Sometimes the professor used the rod as punishment when William drew pictures in class or scuffled with other students.

William didn't like Professor Wallace's strict discipline, or his hickory stick, but he liked the music lessons.

Those first thirty minutes every morning helped him tolerate the rest of each day.

Then came the day that was as black and miserable as the afternoon William hurried home with the guitar.

On this particular morning Professor Wallace surprised everyone by skipping math. He folded his arms and said, "Students, it is time to think about your futures and what you will do with your lives. What plans do you have for your futures?"

One by one the students told what they hoped to be—doctors, lawyers, teachers and preachers. When it was time for William to speak, he summoned his courage and proudly said, "I'm going to be a musician!"

The classroom fell dead silent. The color drained from Professor Wallace's face. He looked as if he would faint. William might as well have said that he planned to be a thief or an assassin.

Everyone stared at William. Professor Wallace leaped from his chair and furiously waved his long, powerful arms in the air. He glared at William while he told him what he thought of musicians.

"Musicians are idlers and wasteful characters who squander their time and energies," Professor Wallace ranted. "They are whiskey drinkers and rounders and they are among the lowest forms of social outcasts—music will most assuredly take you to the gutters!

"We should follow the examples of white Southern gentlemen who look upon music as a parlor accomplishment," the professor continued, "*not* as a means of questionable support." Each time Professor Wallace repeated the word "musician," his face drew up tightly—as if he had just bitten into one of his sour persimmons. The very word seemed to leave a horrible taste in his mouth.

To make matters worst, Professor Wallace wrote a note and insisted that William deliver it to his father.

William walked home from school that day with a note that felt like a hundred-pound weight in his pocket. He walked slow. He took the longest path through the woods. He didn't want to get home any sooner than he had to.

He loved the woods. He loved every single sound

that came from the dense thicket. Even the chattering of the squirrels seemed to have rhythm. The sounds from the whippoorwill and dove usually comforted William and the carefree chirping from the bluebird and goldfinch usually brought a smile to his face. But not today.

Today he could only wonder, *What could be so terribly wrong with enjoying these sounds?* The sounds were music to William. The sounds gave him ideas about making more music. He had ideas, lots of ideas. How could wanting to do this be such a bad thing?

After delaying as long as he could, William plodded up the steps to the cabin. Reverend Handy was sitting at the table reading the Bible. William handed him the note.

Reverend Handy's eyes filled with anger and disappointment, just as they had the day William came home with the guitar.

He slowly raised his eyes from the note to stare at William.

"You forget this nonsense," he said. "You will *not* become a musician.

"I'd rather see you in a hearse. I'd rather follow you to the graveyard than to hear that you've become a musician. Do you understand my words? Letting you become a musician would be just like selling your soul to the devil and watching you trot down to hell on a fast horse in a porcupine saddle. I will not let that happen!"

William bit his bottom lip to hold back the sobs. Bitter tears stung his eyes and a lump in his throat made it impossible to swallow. But it was the piercing pain in his heart that was the most unbearable of all.

William loved and respected his father.

When words finally found their way out, he only could say, "yes, sir."

He heart was saying something different, though.

Just wait—one day I'll show him and everybody else in this town, William silently vowed. *I WILL become a musician!*

A $1.75 Bargain

A YOUNG MAN NAMED JIM TURNER came to town about the time William was finishing at the district school. Turner played the violin better than anyone in Florence had ever heard before. When his bow touched the violin's strings it was magic.

Jim arrived from Memphis, Tennessee and through his eyes and music the people of Florence glimpsed another world. He talked nonstop about Beale Street in Memphis, where people never seemed to sleep and "life was a song from dawn to dawn." He also dressed in all the latest fashions.

William soaked in every word as Jim shared his thrilling tales of life in Memphis.

The more he listened, the more he wanted to see that new kind of life for himself.

He loved Florence and his family, but he could feel the pull of another way of life, a life much more exciting than anything he had ever known.

About the same time, a circus passing through North Alabama found itself stranded in Florence. With no way to get out of town, the bandmaster started teaching music lessons at a barbershop.

William slowly strolled by the shop on the way home from school each day. He peeked through the windows and studied the blackboard chart used by the bandmaster to illustrate playing techniques for several instruments. After peeking at the blackboard for several days, William sat at his desk in school and during class secretly practiced the music techniques he saw on the blackboard.

One warm day the classroom doors and windows were pushed open to catch a breeze. William's big ears perked up. A faint tune was riding on the breeze. It was the voice of an old black plowman, a half mile away.

The old man sang:

A-O OO A-O I wouldn't live in Cair-ro

A-O OO A-O-OO

Instead of hearing the lessons of the day, William wondered what was in the singer's mind. *What was wrong with Cairo? Why wouldn't someone want to live there?* He filed the song's tones and the words away in his mind.

William kept wandering by the barbershop and peeking in the windows until one of the band members noticed him and talked him into buying an old cornet, a small horn that is played somewhat like a trumpet. This instrument had valves on the side instead of on the top like the more modern cornets. It looked odd but since the price was only one dollar and seventy-five cents William couldn't resist. He gave the fellow a quarter and made installment payments on the remaining balance. William loved this old cornet and secretly practiced every chance he got.

He began to practice with the Florence band until his father and Professor Wallace discovered what he was doing. But this time it was too late to do much about it. William was about to finish school, and he was old enough to go off on his own.

Jim Turner remained in Florence and started a band of his own. One afternoon he had a problem and wondered if William could help.

Turner's band had been hired to play at a land sale in nearby Russellville, but the band needed an alto player. Could William fill in?

Turner's problem was William's opportunity.

He skipped school and joined the band. He

earned *eight whole dollars* for the day. It seemed like all the money in the world since he usually earned only three dollars for an entire week of hard labor.

William just knew that his father would be impressed. But just as before, Reverend Handy disapproved. He called the money "tainted wages." He refused to forgive his son and Professor Wallace whipped William with the hickory stick the next day at school.

William wanted the blessing of his parents, but now he realized that they were not going to change their views toward his beloved music. So he decided to go ahead and pursue his dream without their approval.

He attended dances against their wishes, and sang with a quartet that performed until the late hours of night.

He joined the hometown minstrel show that performed comedy skits and music.

William was hooked.

From the first time he stepped on stage in his father's jim-swinger (a Prince Albert style, long-tailed coat worn by musicians) there was no doubt what William intended to do with his life.

Leaving Florence

WILLIAM FINISHED SCHOOL IN FLORENCE, and on September 7, 1892, at the age of eighteen, he left for Birmingham, the big bustling new city to the south.

He chose the fast-growing Birmingham because a family friend encouraged him to come and become a schoolteacher.

William saw it as the perfect chance to work during the day and play his music in the big city by night. William passed the teacher's examination only to discover that some teachers were paid less than twenty-five dollars a month. Laborers made more than that, so instead of teaching,

William went to work for the Howard and Harrison Pipe Works in Bessemer. The job was hard labor but the job paid a dollar and eighty-five cents a day and William had never minded hard working. His job was to pour ladles of molten metal. It made his eyes burn, but he didn't let that stop him.

When he wasn't working at the pipe works, William organized and taught his first brass band and trained musicians from a small string orchestra to read notes. His students nicknamed him "Professor" or "Fess" out of respect for his tremendous knowledge of music. William played the trumpet at one of Birmingham's larger churches and he began showing up at a lot of parties and other events.

Just when William seemed to be headed down the road to success, an economic panic hit and the pipe factory shut down. William's savings dwindled away and he passed the time by walking about the streets of Birmingham. He walked by a saloon one day and heard the music from a quartet singing inside. He walked in to introduce himself and offered to teach the young singers some arrangements his band had used in Florence. One thing led to another and soon William was in business with the singers. The group named themselves the "Lauzetta Quartet."

The quartet became popular in Birmingham but there was little money to be made because of tough times. The group decided that if they were to make it big, they should head for the World's Fair in Chicago. Surely there would be money in a town the size of Chicago.

William had twenty cents and the other quartet members had no money at all. So they met at the freight yards and hopped on a railroad tank car headed for Chicago.

The train's brakeman threw the freeloaders off each time they pulled into a depot. But each time the brakeman turned his head, the determined men hopped right back on board. The exasperated brakeman threatened to toss the group off while the train was moving if they were caught on board again. The fellows had to think fast. They quickly struck up a tune.

The brakeman just as quickly interrupted them. "Why didn't you say you could sing?" He let the men ride in the caboose and serenade the train crew.

The train pulled into the Decatur, Alabama station the next morning. William spotted a group of white women heading toward the Tennessee River for a picnic. He asked if they would be interested in music during the picnic, and they agreed that entertainment would be nice. The women paid the quartet ten dollars.

If it worked in Decatur, it would work in other towns. William and his quartet bounced northward toward Chicago, singing and playing as they went. It kept a little money in their pockets.

Things could have been a lot worse.

In fact, times soon got much worse.

They reached Chicago to discover that the fair had been postponed for a year.

With no place to perform they had to move on, and quick.

St. Louis wasn't too far away. It was a great music town. Right on the Mississippi River. Surely there would be work for a quartet in St. Louis.

When they arrived, they found times as hard in St. Louis as everywhere else. But to make matters worse, it seemed that every music group in America had the same idea as William's group. Quartets from all over the world were stranded in this town. The Lauzetta Quartet soon disbanded.

William was as alone as he ever had been and in a city he knew nothing about. He worked odd jobs to survive. He was plagued with lice so badly that he threw away his infested shirt and underclothes and walked the streets with only a rumpled overcoat and tattered trousers. Many nights he slept in a vacant lot or on the cobblestones of the Mississippi River levee. He felt alone, but he wasn't. There were almost a thousand other homeless men in St. Louis, black and white, struggling to just stay alive.

William was unshaven, dirty and dressed in rags. He was hungry and felt lucky to get a bread crust for a meal. One night he walked by a saloon in the white part of town and was drawn in by a familiar tune. He shuffled inside and asked if he might share a few songs. He impressed the crowd so much that they took up a collection to help him as he went on his way.

That night as he lay on the river levee under the stars, arguing voices drifted through his mind.

Go home, said one. *Go home where you have friends and family.*

I told you so, said another. *I told you that you should have become a minister like your father.*

No! You will not return home, said yet another. *You will fight it out in spite of your troubles.*

That final voice won the debate.

William did not return home.

He used the money collected at the saloon to buy a change of clothing and jumped on a freight train leaving St. Louis.

Bitter Times And Better Times

WILLIAM JUMPED OFF THE TRAIN when it stopped in Evansville, Indiana.

He found work on a crew paving the city streets.

He began feeling better now that he had money to buy food and to freshen up.

During that summer of 1894 he landed a job with a band aboard the *W. F. Nesbitt*, a steam boat that carried tourists between Evansville and the Civil War battlefield at Shiloh on the Tennessee River.

The riverboat brought William within fifty miles of his hometown and each week he planned to run home for a short visit with his mother, but something always seemed to get in the way.

When he got back home from the last summer trip he still had not visited his mother. At the door lay a telegram: "Come at once if you want to see your mother alive." William couldn't believe the words that he re-read the note through tear-filled eyes.

He left immediately but he was too late.

Church bells were tolling when he reached Florence. He met the crowd as they returned from the cemetery where they had just buried his mother.

A young Elizabeth V. Price

William traveled back to Henderson, Kentucky (a community just across the Ohio River from Evansville) with a heavy heart.

He threw himself into his work and caught on with several brass bands. The groups entertained at lavish barbecues for the wealthy citizens of Henderson. William began to think of himself as a professional musician—no longer a hobo or drifting laborer, but a musician!

Lots of good things began to happen in Henderson . . . and the best thing of all was named Elizabeth V. Price. William met Elizabeth on Emancipation Day in Held's Park where festivities were held to celebrate the end of slavery. Elizabeth was lovely and William could not take his eyes off of her. He had hoped to find someone just like this special person and she even shared the name of his beloved mother. Deep down he knew that Elizabeth, *Lizzie*, would one day become Mrs. W.C. Handy.

Things got better still when a letter arrived from a young musician friend. Elmore Dodd and William had crossed paths while traveling and Dodd had ended up in Chicago. The letter invited William to come to Chicago and join Mahara's Minstrels. The group needed someone to play the cornet and William was their choice. The salary would be only six dollars a week plus "cakes." That meant food would be provided. William jumped at the opportunity. The money wasn't great, but he would be fed, get to travel, and, best of all, he would be surrounded by some of the finest black musicians of the day.

Lizzie was against the move. Her family and friends didn't think much of minstrels. Such traveling musicians seemed like a shady bunch who loved whiskey and fast living.

William loved Elizabeth, but he knew what he had to do.

Mahara's Minstrels

ON AUGUST 6, 1896 W.C. Handy joined Mahara's Minstrels in Chicago, Illinois. The decision to join the group changed his life.

Soon after William arrived in Chicago, the bass violin player left the show and William stepped right into his spot. His salary climbed to seven dollars a week. He began to train quartets for the show and even bought himself a spanking new C.G. Conn gold-plated trumpet. He had come a long way since the days of playing the old one dollar and seventy-five cent cornet with the valves on the side.

William took on extra duties of arranging orchestrations and becoming the cornet soloist. Others noticed his talents. His salary grew and he bought several fancy outfits. His new clothes, hat, and spats to cover his shoe tops all were cut from the same bolt of rich brown cloth. He looked good! He bought a watch fob, an umbrella strap, and a couple of diamonds to top off the outfit. He was a dandy indeed. People noticed when Mr. W.C. Handy walked down the street, and whispered about him. William heard their whispers and he liked what he heard, "Look at that handsome fellow. Why just look at his eyes and that smile!"

William, a young and dapper dandy

The Minstrels' day began at 11:45 when they lined up at the theatre and paraded through the streets. They did it every time they visited a new town to drum up business for their nightly shows. Four-horse carriages lead the parade carrying the show managers decked out in silk hats and jeweled smiles.

Next came a carriage full of the show's stars. The "walking gents" followed. This group included comedians, singers and acrobats. The drum major followed the walkers and he put on quite a show! He pranced with his baton, using his twirling stick to toss a revolving bicycle wheel into the air and then retrieve it with flawless skill. The drum major usually stole the show as all eyes followed his every move. The Mahara's Minstrels actually had two drum majors. These two characters impressed the crowd by not only twirling one baton, but by tossing the batons back and forth to each other as they marched. The boys with banners were the final addition to the parade. They mingled through the procession and their banners described features for the nightly show.

The entertainers enjoyed a few hours of free time during the afternoons before the minstrel show started at 7:30 p.m.

The minstrel show was something like a circus event, always beginning with the announcer stepping onto the stage. He was all decked out, usually sporting blue silk and lace and silk stovepipe hat.

"LA-DEEEZ AND GENTLEMEN, we've come out tonight to give you a pleasing entertainment. With bones on the right and tambourines on the left we'll proceed with the overture. Gentlemen, be seated!"

There were comedy skits with lots of silly pranks, dancing, a conventional orchestra, and singers.

This was the life for William! In spite of long demanding hours, he knew that music was his life. He loved every minute of his day. He enjoyed meeting the talented people of the minstrel show and he learned from everyone who crossed his path. He also practiced four to six hours each day on his cornet.

William continued to listen to the sounds around him, just as he had when he was a boy in Florence. But the sounds of Chicago were not like those of the fields and forests of Florence, Alabama.

These were city sounds. Honking horns. Horses clopping on paved streets. Horseless carriages putting and popping along. Shouts and calls of workers, and the clatter of machinery.

One cold night he heard a washerwoman singing. She took her husband's frozen shirts from the clothes-line and in a moanful voice she sang, "Yo' clothes looks lonesome hangin' on de line." That same night he tried to reproduce the exact tone of her voice on his violin so that he might later use the sounds in his songs.

While William was having the time of his life traveling with the show, his beloved Elizabeth wondered what was becoming of their romance. She waited back in Henderson, Kentucky, and the two rarely saw each other. Most of their courting was done through letters. William had proposed and then asked for Elizabeth's hand in marriage by writing to her father.

They were married on July 19, 1898. A two-week vacation followed and then William was antsy to rejoin the minstrel show. He thought Elizabeth would be excited to join him on the road.

He was wrong. Elizabeth just couldn't see herself traveling with "show people." She shook her head gloomily and begged William to settle down in Henderson. She wanted him to take a steady job, maybe go into the grocery business. This time William shook his head. The grocery business didn't appeal to him at all. So Elizabeth remained in Henderson while her new husband traveled from town to town with Mahara's Minstrels.

In those days, smallpox was a dreaded disease. Many people died from smallpox. It was contagious and sometime spread rapidly through whole towns.

Anytime a case of smallpox was discovered, the infected person was kept away from others until they were well. Or until they died and were buried.

It was that dread disease that changed the off and on, road and home relationship of Elizabeth and William.

Just before a show was about to begin one afternoon, the local doctor showed up and announced at the public square that one of the performers had smallpox, and that if the minstrels didn't leave town immediately the whole troupe would be lynched!

Mahara's Minstrels wasted no time getting out of town.

Word of the smallpox reached the next town before the minstrels did, and they weren't welcome there either.

It was the same stop after stop.

No one wanted entertainers who might be bringing smallpox.

No one else in the troupe got sick, but it didn't matter.

No one wanted to book Mahara's Minstrels.

They had to do something to get work, so they decided to go to Havana, Cuba.

William assured Elizabeth that Havana would be different than the road shows. He begged her to join him. Besides, he argued, two could live as cheaply as one.

Elizabeth gave in to his arguments and all the troubles of the past seem to fade away when the two entered the Havana harbor. Tears filled Elizabeth's eyes as she marveled at the spectacular view. Together they witnessed the beauty of the rising sun and the splendors of the shimmering purple sea. Perhaps things would be different on this island. The Handy's enjoyed afternoons driving about the city and the surrounding countryside. They browsed the small shops and bought special mementos like unusual fans, old coins and jewelry.

It was on this island that William learned he was going to be a father. Life was good. And it was going to get a lot better.

The Sweetest Words

THE MINSTRELS RETURNED FROM CUBA after the smallpox scare finally settled down. They performed across North Alabama, including Huntsville, only 60 miles from Florence where William's father still lived.

William had not been to Florence since his mother died, and he was completely caught off guard when he saw the face he knew so well among the afternoon Huntsville crowd.

William couldn't believe his eyes.

There sat Reverend Handy!

His father!

The crowd enjoyed the show tremendously that afternoon, patting the performers on the back and showering the band with kind words. William suddenly singled out that all familiar preacher voice from all the others in the crowd.

Reverend Handy was talking about his son.

William was struck speechless by his father's words to the strangers in the crowd.

They were not words of bitterness or disappointment.

In fact, they were exactly the opposite.

"The leader of the band is *my* son!" Reverend Handy was smiling from ear to ear while bragging to anyone that would listen. His expression said it all. He was *proud* of his son. William's father looked as if he were about to burst with pride! Reverend Handy remained for the evening show too and when the curtain fell, he took William's hand in his own leathered hands and said, "Sonny, I haven't been in a show since I professed religion. I enjoyed it. I am very proud of you and forgive you for becoming a musician."

William thought he would never hear those words, and, he thought, they were the sweetest words he had ever heard. But hear them he did, and his heart swelled with joy. His father was *proud* of him!

The show moved to Florence the next day and again was a big hit. Large crowds attended every performance. Even Professor Wallace came to offer his approval of William's accomplishments.

William made an important decision while the

minstrels were playing in North Alabama.

He decided to quit the show and remain in Florence since his first child was on the way. Lucile Handy was born on June 29, 1900.

Even with a new child, life in the small town was

The young and growing Handy family

dull after traveling with the minstrels.

The minstrels had taken William from Cuba to California and from Canada to Mexico. He had performed with some of the most talented black singers and musicians of the time. While some considered minstrel shows to be filled with lazy, dishonest characters, William knew better. He had lived with these gifted entertainers and found that many of them regularly sent money back home to pay for the education of family members or to care for elderly parents. It was done while supporting growing families of their own. But most importantly, work in the minstrel shows had been responsible for William's return to the good graces of his family and the people of the town he loved so dearly. They wanted his shows and now they respected his work.

That September, William joined the faculty of the Agricultural and Mechanical College located near Huntsville. He led the school's band, the orchestra and the vocal music program. The teaching job provided the first real home that Williams's young family had ever had. A second daughter, Katherine, soon came along.

Mahara's Minstrels kept asking William to rejoin the group and kept offering him more money until he could no longer resist. But just for a year.

After that he took a job directing a Knights of Pythias band in Clarksdale, Mississippi, not far from the Mississippi River and less than a hundred miles south of Memphis.

It would be another life-changing move.

Hearing The New Sound

THE KNIGHTS OF PYTHIAS BAND played in towns others than Clarksville. But the travel was never as much as with Mahara's Minstrels.

And that was just fine with Elizabeth.

Still, the band traveled to play for different groups around the state.

One day while waiting for a train to take him to the band's next performance, William noticed a black man plunking on his guitar. This fellow wore rags for clothes and William could see his feet through holes in his battered shoes. Sadness hung on the old man's face from a lifetime of hard living. As he played the guitar, the man pressed a knife on the strings and made a sound that William would never forget.

The words of the sad man's songs were unforgettable too:

"Goin' where the Southern cross' the Dog."

William didn't know exactly what the words meant, but he liked them. They stirred something deep in his soul.

The man sang about traveling the railways and the same simple line was repeated three times. It was the strangest and most hauntingly beautiful music William had ever heard.

But the sounds reminded him of something.

They conjured up strains of the old folk music he had listened to growing up in Florence. The sounds wouldn't leave his mind.

They made William think about the way Southern blacks sang about everything. About their work. Their play. Their heartaches and their troubles.

The oddest things became subjects for their songs and they pecked out the tune on any old thing they could find that produced a musical sound or rhythmic beat.

William remembered his love for creating music, with a comb, a cow horn, even an old jawbone. He realized he had pushed that sort of music to the back of his mind while focusing on "dressed-up music" from books.

Listening to this train station musician forced William to question what he believed about music...about what was "worthwhile" music and what wasn't.

He had trained himself to think that the important stuff came from books. Yet these simple sounds could not be found in books. These songs had been born out of hard times and suffering.

All of his technical training in music had caused William to look down on the back street musicians. He had thought that their music was just something for common folk.

He began to wonder if he had been wrong.

Not long after his encounter with the train station guitar player, William and his band were playing for a white audience in Cleveland, Mississippi. Cleveland is a delta town about forty miles south of Clarksdale.

A voice called out from the audience, "Play some of your native music." William led his well-trained group in a sophisticated old Southern melody. The crowd responded with a half-hearted round of applause and then asked if the band would allow a local black trio to play a few songs. William thought it was a great chance to take a break and gladly handed the stage over to the local street musicians who simply played for handouts.

The trio struck up an old song that seemed to have no clear beginning or ending. It just started and wandered around some.

The sounds from the group's battered guitar, mandolin and a beat up bass made William turn his head to listen more closely.

As the song trailed off to a close, William watched in amazement as the crowd went wild. They stomped their feet and threw silver dollars at the raggedy musicians. *This was what the people wanted*, William thought, *and it wasn't his fancy music.*

The simple music touched a spot deep inside the listeners, causing them to sway and move to the rhythm.

W.C. Handy was proud to call himself a musician and composer.

He was proud of his musical talent, and knew that he was better than most.

But that night in Cleveland, Mississippi, those country boys taught William something about music that he never could have learned in school.

Their music had reached deep inside and touched souls. People identified these sounds with suffering. But the sounds actually eased their pain and made them feel good all over.

William noticed something else that night. The street musicians collected more money when coins were tossed at intermission than his band earned the entire night. Not only did the people love these sounds, but there was money to be made—lots and lots of money!

He thought of the raggedy old fellow at the train station and hundreds of others he had seen in his travels, but paid less attention to.

William quickly wrote down tunes that he could recall from these street singers. The more he wrote, the more ideas kept popping into his head. He wrote down ideas for tunes nonstop. Sometimes he scribbled notes under dim lights while traveling on lurching trains or in his room by the light of a coal-oil lamp. It was hard on his eyes, but he had coped with poor eyesight practically all his life.

William's band began performing the new songs. They were instantly popular and requests for show bookings flooded in.

The places that wanted them most weren't always the nicest ones, but the songs were always a success and the money was good!

Their music and success pulled William northward, back toward Memphis.

It was the place William dreamed about as a boy. It was the place where Jim Turner had come from when he wandered into Florence, Alabama, and filled young William's head with stories of Beale Street and juke joints that never closed.

It was the place where William's life would change forever.

Birth of the Blues

IT WAS THE FALL OF 1909 when William and his band arrived in Memphis. They spent a lot of time at a musician's hangout named Pee Wee's Saloon. Pee Wee's was on Beale Street, the place of William's boyhood dreams.

The band caught on quickly. They made a lot of money. Everyone seemed to like their new music...music from the sounds of everyday life, from the woods, and fields, and back streets of Chicago.

Pretty soon, the band was hired to create a special campaign tune for Edward "Boss" Crump, who was running for mayor of Memphis. The tune had to be lively enough to catch everyone's attention, but no words were to be written.

When he got the assignment, William immediately thought about a rhythm that he often heard being played by the black roustabouts and honky-tonk piano players.

He thought of how black musicians expressed their feelings in song as if they were talking to themselves. Although Mr. Crump and his staff only heard the tune without words, William had jokingly written words to the tune and gave them to visiting bands:

Mr. Crump won't 'low no easy riders here
Mr. Crump won't 'low no easy riders here
We don't care what Mr. Crump don't 'low
We gon' to bar'l-house anyhow -
Mr. Crump can go and catch hisself some air!

The words mocked Boss Crump's uppity attitude and his campaign against freeloaders.

The tune was an instant a hit. Mr. Crump was elected as mayor. And Handy became a celebrity.

William published the campaign song under a new title, *Memphis Blues.*

With its publication, a new kind of music was born.

Part of this new sound that William had created was his capturing in music the slurs of black people's voices as they sang their songs of trouble and sorrow. He did it by imitating the sound with musical instruments.

The world came to know the sound as *the blues.*

Immediately William's band was swamped with

calls. Blacks and whites both loved the blues! Memphis couldn't get enough of the new sounds created by W.C. Handy. People crowded into the nightclubs every time the blues were played.

Things moved so fast it was hard for W.C. to keep up.

William was just sure he had a hit on his hands and he needed a company to publish his *Memphis Blues.*

In 1912 he paid a company $32 to print one thousand copies of the song, plus one more dollar for the copyright fee.

The copies were sent to music stores but each time William looked on the shelves, stacks of his music were still there.

How could he have been so wrong.

Everyone said they loved his music.

Big crowds came to hear him play.

Why wouldn't they buy the music, he wondered.

He could not figure it out.

Day after day he visited the music stores, and day after day things were just the same.

Stacks of *Memphis Blues* stood tall on the shelves.

William was devastated.

A Hard Lesson

ONE DAY WHEN he could stand it no longer, William went to the publishers office to see why they thought his music was not selling.

The publisher told William that the customers thought the piece was too hard to play, and that was why they weren't buying it.

William didn't like the news.

But what could he do. *He had*, he decided, *made a mistake*. He would make the best of it and move on.

When the publisher offered to reimburse William for his printing costs, plus a small profit, William gladly accepted.

And when the publisher offered to give back the dollar William paid to have *Memphis Blues* copyrighted, he gladly took that too. But by doing it, the rights to the music were given to the publisher too. The swap meant William would earn no royalties (or profits) if the music ever sold. Right then it didn't seem to matter much. The publisher said no one wanted to buy it anyway.

Time passed by and something just didn't seem right to William.

Memphis Blues was being played all over town. Everyone loved the song.

How could they be playing his song if they thought it was too hard, and they hadn't bought the music? he wondered.

How could they just start playing the piece without any music, he wanted to know.

They did have the music, he soon discovered.

They had bought it! Lots of people had bought it! Thousands of them!

The publisher had tricked William.

The publisher had secretly printed several thousand copies of William's song, not just 1,000 copies that they had discussed. The song had been selling like hotcakes! With so many copies printed, the publisher kept the shelves full and made William think it was not selling. The publisher made a lot of money with his mean, dishonest trick, and William made nothing.

What could William do?

Tell the publisher he knew what had happened, and demand that the company give the song back?

There were no laws to protect him or other songwriters. There was nothing he could do.

William decided to put his resentment behind him and look to the future. He would remember his mistake and come out better the next time.

In fact, he already had another idea...

Now that he knew that people really were buying his music, he had lots of ideas for more songs.

The ideas were much more important than worrying about a sneaky publisher.

William was not getting any of the money pouring in from the sales of his *Memphis Blues.* But it made him happy to hear the popular song played over and over on Beale Street and throughout all of Memphis.

When big conventions came to the city, William and his band often were the featured act. Every time they played, they grew more famous.

Visitors to Memphis took the music back home with them.

Soon, his new sounds were spreading to every corner of America, and beyond.

People couldn't seem to get enough, and that made William happy.

He was beginning to understand just what the blues meant to the rest of the country.

William was forty years old, and the Handy family now consisted of four rambunctious children. They were a happy bunch living in a small cottage on Janette Street. They planted an orchard, flowers and a vegetable garden. It was a good place to be.

But with four children it was so loud and rowdy that William could hardly think. As William tried to concentrate on his song writing his children fought to sit on their father's lap and use his legs for teeterboards.

William loved his family. But he was on a mission. And as hard as he tried, he couldn't get the music to come with his children gathered around his feet.

He desperately wanted another hit. He wanted it to be the new kind of music that he had captured in *Memphis Blues.* He wanted it to be a hit that would make up for the loss of the *Memphis Blues.* He wanted to prove that *Memphis Blues* wasn't just a one-time piece of luck. He wanted to prove to himself that he really had found a new kind of music, a kind of music that rose up from the low end of life, and that captured the attention of everyone all the way to the highest end of life.

He thought he had it figured out.

But there was no way to know for sure until he

did it again.

He had to write more songs.

He had to play them and see the expression on peoples' faces.

Only then would he know for sure.

William decided to take a break from the noisy ruckus and rent a room in the Beale Street section of town. It would be noisy there, too, but the street sounds had always been his inspiration.

William sat alone in the little Beale Street room. Around him were saloons filled with piano thumpers, rowdy pool hall crowds, and street roustabouts. He closed his eyes and a thousand memories flooded his mind as familiar sounds from nearby saloons floated on the air.

He drifted back to the painful days in St. Louis when he was penniless, unshaven, and hungry. He saw himself on that night many years earlier, standing at the door of a St. Louis saloon without a shirt under his thin, frayed coat, and praying that they would let him play for just a few coins.

He remembered a woman from those long-ago days who was trying but failing to mend her broken heart by drinking lots of whiskey. He remembered the words she mumbled over and over as she stumbled along the dimly lit St. Louis street. "Ma man's got a heart like a rock cast in de sea."

William would always remember that the blues comes from aching hearts, not from books or fancy music.

He also knew there was a special kind of music in the phrases and dialect of black people. Their phrases held feelings better than well-chosen, proper English. William worked to capture their phrases and distinct dialect in musical notes.

The scenes of St. Louis shifted to the distant sounds from cotton fields, railroads, and the river levee. He heard the singers' natural slurring between notes and decided that this would be part of his new music too.

And he thought of the many nights when he slept outdoors on cobblestones near towns that did not allow black people. He remembered the last thoughts that crossed his weary mind as his eyes closed for sleep . . ."I hate to see de evenin' sun go down."

Soon, those very words flowed from his pen.

When he was finished, he gave the words a name.

It was the *St. Louis Blues.*

After soaking in the sounds from Beale Street and dredging up old memories from his hard times, William wrote *St. Louis Blues* after just one evening at the piano.

He loved it.

He couldn't wait to try it out. It would be the ultimate test.

William left Beale Street, rounded up his band, and went straight to a popular nightspot.

As the band started to play, William knew there was no turning back, no more fine tuning, no more tinkering with melody or words.

Either the crowd would like the music or they wouldn't.

Their reaction would tell him. Either he had captured a new sound. Or he was just another better-than-average musician who had gotten lucky once.

Was *Memphis Blues* his one moment of luck?

Or was it the beginning of something wonderful?

William's eyes eagerly scanned the dance floor as the band played the tune for the first time.

He searched every face for a sign.

In an instant, William no longer had to search the crowd's faces. He could feel their energy. There seemed to be an electrical current flowing through them. The dancers came to life and kicked up their heels higher than ever.

They loved *St. Louis Blues*!

He had done it!

The world didn't know it right then, but William did.

He knew there were more songs where that one came from, and he intended to write them just as fast as he could.

At the end of the evening, the band piled into cabs and followed William home.

The night had seemed almost too good to be true.

The group was ready to celebrate the birth of the new blues.

Mrs. Handy had another idea.

She was a little more than fed up.

She opened the door with one hand on her hip and the other holding a rolling pin.

Her husband had been away for the past twenty-four hours and had neglected to state exactly where he was going or what he was doing.

The boys in the band howled with laughter as they watched William sweet talk Lizzie into putting away her rolling pin.

Finally William decided the best thing would be to stay home and make up with Lizzie, and just let the rest of the band go out and celebrate their leader's new hit.

And that is exactly what happened on that fateful night in 1914.

A famous W.C. Handy in New York with his family

Epilogue

EVENTUALLY W.C. HANDY DID GET A CHANCE to celebrate the success of the St. Louis Blues and many other hits.

His first two hits, *Memphis Blues* and the *St. Louis Blues* were written while William was immersed in the sounds of Beale Street. In 1917 he paid tribute to that one-of-a-kind place and published the *Beale Street Blues.*

The song was inspired by the music of a Beale Street piano player. Something about the player's rhythm wasn't quite right. William walked into the smoke filled café and asked the musician about his strange way of playing the piano. The poor fellow explained that he was simply dog-tired! This happy-go-lucky piano thumper had to play from seven at night until seven in the morning. His style was created as he rested one hand and played with the other so he could hold up to play for twelve hours straight!

An overflow crowd gathers for the dedication of W.C. Handy Park in Memphis, Tennessee, March 29, 1931

Usually a blues singer fills in musical gaps with words like "Oh, Baby" or "Oh, Lawdy." The worn out piano player was William's inspiration to include such musical breaks into his compositions.

Beale Street Blues used that same funny rhythm with breaks and it was a huge success.

The next few years witnessed a string of steady hits from W.C. Handy.

By 1931 William and his family had moved to New York where he ran a publishing company and wrote songs.

On March 14, 1931 he received a letter from Memphis, Tennessee. A vacant lot was being converted into a city park, and to his surprise, the park would bear his name!

William felt honored, and agreed to return to Memphis for the dedication ceremony.

The dedication was on Sunday, March 29, 1931. The parade was so long that it took hours for the procession to reach the speaker's stand. William rode in the head vehicle, smiling and tipping his silk hat to the crowds. From time to time he brushed a tear away from happy eyes.

Famous citizens and government officials accompanied William to the speakers' stand.

Eloquent speeches were made praising William's accomplishments and thanking him for his role in establishing Beale Street as the birthplace of the blues.

As the speakers offered their speeches of praise, William's mind drifted back in time.

He thought of the fiery words that his father had shouted when William announced to his class that he wanted to be a musician: "You are trotting down to Hell on a fast horse in a porcupine saddle." *If this was true,* he thought, *then he had ridden with a song on his lips that warmly echoed in his heart.*

William thought back to the prediction of his teacher, Professor Wallace, that "music would bring him to the gutter." *Yes*, William agreed, *he had often slept in street gutters. But it had also been music that lifted him from the gutters.*

W.C. Handy, as William came to be known, lived to experience the rewards of hard times and hard work. His songs continued to enjoy success around the world and his name became recognized as a leader in the music industry.

He and a man named Harry Pace operated the Pace & Handy Publishing Company. William's younger brother, Charles, moved to New York to help with the publishing business.

While William was always the musical star, the business was not always great. Sometimes there were more bills than money to pay them and William struggled to keep the business going.

Just when his business was at its worst, William got more bad news. It was his eyes. They always gave him problems. Even as a boy he squinted in bright sunlight. Then there was the baseball hitting him in the eye, and the iron furnace job that made his eyes burn. After years of reading by dim light, William knew his vision was worsening. But now he could hardly see.

Doctors operated on his eyes and brought back his sight. But in 1943 a fall from a subway platform left him permanently blind. The determined composer quickly learned Braille so that he could continue writing his music. Several of his songs were published in Braille.

In his final years William spent time visiting old friends, writing new songs, and traveling.

His beloved Lizzie died in 1937. They had shared a life of ups and downs for almost fifty years. Their marriage produced five healthy children and they buried one child in infancy. That child was named *Florence* in honor of William's beloved home town.

In 1954 William married fifty-one year old Miss Irma Louise Logan. He was eighty years old and Miss Logan—his secretary and constant companion for many years—had served as "his eyes" when he could no longer see. One year later William suffered a stroke. After that he could no longer walk. He traveled in a a wheelchair.

His 84th birthday was celebrated at the Waldorf-Astoria in New York City. More than 800 people came to wish him well.

Four months later, on March 28, 1958, William died of acute bronchial pneumonia at the age of 84.

An estimated 150,000 stood along the funeral

route in his honor, as the hearse slowly made its way to Woodlawn Cemetery in the Bronx, New York.

Mrs. Irma Logan Handy, with W.C. on his 83rd birthday

W.C. Handy continues to live on through his music. Each year thousands of travelers visit his birthplace in Florence to celebrate his life and his legacy. Mr. Handy's hometown pays tribute to him during the weeklong W. C. Handy Music Festival.

The park in Memphis still bears his name and his music continues to drift from Beale Street and anywhere else where the blues are played.

The small cabin from Handy's Hill is now the W. C. Handy Museum located in Florence. The museum displays a collection of personal papers and artifacts, William's trumpet, his piano and handwritten sheet music are located here as well. The W.C. Handy Library is on the museum grounds and is a valuable resource center for black history and culture.

In 1969, W.C. Handy was honored posthumously (after his death) by the United States Postal Service with a commemorative stamp. The Post Master General of the U.S. noted that just before his death at the age of 84 Mr. Handy spoke to a group of school children. Patting his trumpet, William told the children:

"Life is like this trumpet. If you don't put anything into it, you don't get anything out. And that's the truth."

William Christopher Handy lived that truth all his life.

William Christopher Handy

Nov. 16, 1873 Born in a log cabin on Handy's Hill in Florence, Alabama. His parents were Reverend Charles B. and Elizabeth Brewer Handy.

September 7, 1892 Moves from Florence to Birmingham to become a teacher. Instead, he becomes a laborer at Howard and Harrison Pipe Works in Bessemer.

Summer of 1894 William's mother, Elizabeth Brewer Handy, dies

Handy plays aboard the W.F. Nesbitt excursion steamer operating between Evansville, Indiana and Shiloh battlefield in Tennessee.

August 6, 1896 Joins the Mahara's Minstrels in Chicago, Illinois

July 19, 1898 Marries Elizabeth V. Price in Henderson, Kentucky

Summer, 1900 Moves back to Florence for a brief time; his music is finally accepted there by family and friends

September 1900 - 1902 Serves as faculty member at the Agricultural and Mechanical college near Huntsville, Alabama

Fall 1909 Writes campaign song for Edward "Boss" Crump in Memphis, Tennessee. The song, originally titled *Mr. Crump*, was later released as the *Memphis Blues.* It was the first of many blues written by Handy that year.

1913 Founds his own publishing company

1914 *St. Louis Blues* written

Handy family moves to Janette Street in Memphis, Tennessee

1917 *Beale Street Blues* written

Moves his publishing company to New York and partners with Harry H. Pace to form the firm of Pace & Handy.

1928 Handy sponsored and conducted a sixty-voice chorus and a thirty-piece orchestra at Carnegie Hall in a musical history (tribute) of the Negro

March 29, 1931 W.C. Handy Park dedicated in

Memphis, Tennessee

1925 Shares his memories on the birth of the blues in a publication entitled *Blues—An Anthology*

1928 Sponsors and conducts a sixty-voice choir and thirty-six piece orchestra at Carnegie Hall in a historical musical tribute to the Negro

March 29, 1931 W.C. Handy Park dedicated in Memphis, Tennessee

1937 Wife Elizabeth dies

1938 W.C.Handy's *Collection of Negro Spirituals* published

Nat "King" Cole stars as W.C. Handy in the film *"St. Louis Blues"*

W.C. Handy Tribute at Carnegie Hall

1939-1940 Handy is recognized as a leading contributor to American culture at the New York World's Fair

1940 Regains ownership of *Memphis Blues* after copyright laws are written

1941 Handy publishes his autobiography, *Father of the Blues*

1954 Handy marries second wife, Irma Louise Logan, at the age of 80

1955 Suffers a stroke and is confined to a wheelchair

1958 Still a very popular figure, Handy's 84th birthday party held at the Waldorf-Astoria with more than 800 people attending

March 28, 1958 Handy dies of acute bronchial pneumonia at the age of 84. He had written more that 40 songs that were classified as "blues." He had also written many sacred songs. He was buried in Woodlawn Cemetery in Bronx, New York. Many noted people attending the funeral service and an estimated 150,000 people stood along the funeral route.

1979 Blues Foundation begins the "Handy Awards"—the highest recognition given to blues artists

1993 Inducted into Alabama Music Hall of Fame

About the Author

Alice Yeager grew up in Lauderdale County, Alabama—the home of W.C. Handy. She lives on Shoals Creek and listens to many of the same sounds of nature that inspired young Handy. She has been a classroom teacher, guidance counselor and curriculum specialist. Alice earned a Master's degree in Guidance and Counseling, an Ed.S. in Early Childhood and a Doctorate in Educational Leadership from the University of Alabama at Birmingham.

She has been happily married to her high school sweetheart (Tim) for 24 years. They live in Killen, Alabama with eight active dogs and three extremely persnickety, (but cuddly) cats.

Other Alabama Roots Biographies Available From Seacoast Publishing

Henry Aaron: Dream Chaser by Roz Morris
Hugo Black: Justice For All by Roz Morris
Paul Bryant:Football Legend by Sylvia B. Williams
Sam Dale: Alabama Pioneer by Tom Bailey
Daniel Pratt: Alabama's Great Builder by Tom Bailey
Emma Sansom: Confederate Hero by Margie Ross
Julia Tutwiler: Alabama Crusader by Roz Morris

Coming in the fall, 2002
Rosa Parks: Mother of the Civil Rights Movement
A.G. Gaston: Visionary Businessman
Jesse Owens: World's Fastest Human

To order more copies of this or other Alabama Roots biographies, send 8.95 (includes postage) per book to:
Seacoast Publishing
P.O. Box 26492
Birmingham, AL 35260

Please print on your order the name and address where you wish the books to be shipped. Allow 15 days for delivery.
Orders also may be placed by telephone by calling 205.979.2909.